THE U.S. HOUSE OF REPRESENTATIVES

Bill McAuliffe

Creative Education ★ Creative Paperbacks

TABLE OF CONTENTS

★ ★ ★

REFERENCE

In 1798, the United States House of Representatives was not quite 10 years old, and some of its members hadn't yet learned good manners.

THE U.S. HOUSE OF REPRESENTATIVES

Heated debates were common. One day, Vermont representative Matthew Lyon spat tobacco juice in the face of Connecticut's Roger Griswold. Griswold stayed calm at the time. But two weeks later, Griswold saw Lyon alone at his desk and clubbed him with a hickory cane. Lyon grabbed a pair of iron fireplace tongs and whacked Griswold. Soon, other members of the House were shoving and hitting one another with sticks on the House floor and in the hallways. Such physical assaults—and even duels with pistols—marked government by the people in the early days. Today, neither guns nor tobacco juice are allowed in chambers. But there are still plenty of fights, as parties battle one another over legislation, using words as their weapons.

Griswold attacked Lyon after the House voted not to expel Lyon for the spitting incident.

NUMBER OF REPRESENTATIVES PER STATE, 1789

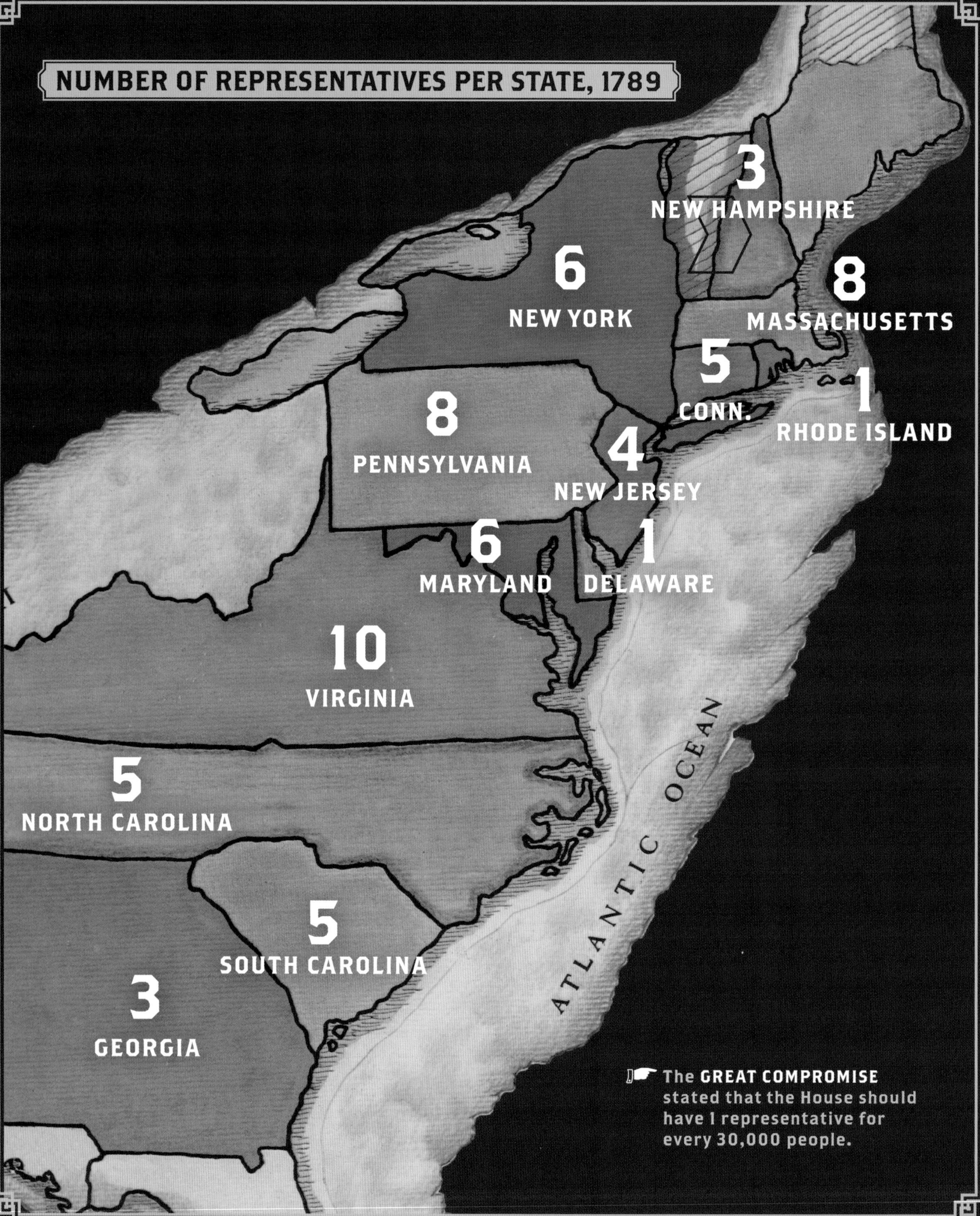

3 NEW HAMPSHIRE

6 NEW YORK

8 MASSACHUSETTS

5 CONN.

1 RHODE ISLAND

8 PENNSYLVANIA

4 NEW JERSEY

6 MARYLAND

1 DELAWARE

10 VIRGINIA

5 NORTH CAROLINA

5 SOUTH CAROLINA

3 GEORGIA

ATLANTIC OCEAN

The **GREAT COMPROMISE** stated that the House should have 1 representative for every 30,000 people.

CHAPTER 1

BUILDING THE HOUSE

THE U.S. HOUSE OF REPRESENTATIVES

When the delegates to the Constitutional convention in 1787 were designing the government of the new country, they started with the group of elected lawmakers. It was crucial to begin there, because they wanted to make sure that laws would be made by representatives of the people rather than by a single executive.

But what, exactly, should that lawmaking body look like? William Patterson of New Jersey suggested one made up of a representative from each state. The state government would choose its own representative. This would ensure that all states had equal say in the decision-making process. Of course, states with big populations, such as Virginia, objected. They were growing quickly and thought they deserved more representation, in keeping with their larger populations. Edmund Randolph of Virginia

GEORGE WASHINGTON

★ It was the House that decided the president should be addressed as "Mr. President." ★

BUILDING THE HOUSE

proposed having two houses in Congress, with membership in each house based on population. The difference would be that representatives in one house would be chosen by the people, and those in the other house would be chosen by legislatures in each state.

After six weeks of debate, Connecticut delegates Roger Sherman and Oliver Ellsworth offered what is now known as the Great Compromise. This deal called for two houses. The first house became the U.S. Senate, with two members elected from each state. The other became the House of Representatives, with proportional representation based on population.

Because of its makeup, the House has always offered a sense of government that is closer to the people. In its first session, the House opened its doors to the public. The Senate remained closed for six more years. Until 1837, House members wore hats on the floor, which was considered a mark of informality. They removed their fashionable headwear only while speaking. When the first Speaker of the House appointed a sergeant-at-arms in 1789, he equipped him with a **mace**. This was a precaution against fights that were expected to break out—and sometimes did. It was the House that decided the president should be addressed as "Mr. President." This beat out the more royal-sounding titles of "His High Mightiness" (favored by George Washington, the

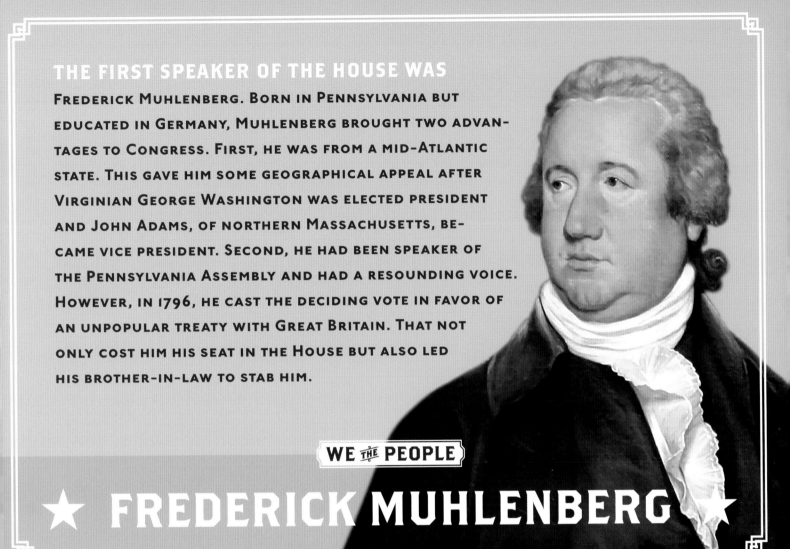

THE FIRST SPEAKER OF THE HOUSE WAS

FREDERICK MUHLENBERG. BORN IN PENNSYLVANIA BUT EDUCATED IN GERMANY, MUHLENBERG BROUGHT TWO ADVANTAGES TO CONGRESS. FIRST, HE WAS FROM A MID-ATLANTIC STATE. THIS GAVE HIM SOME GEOGRAPHICAL APPEAL AFTER VIRGINIAN GEORGE WASHINGTON WAS ELECTED PRESIDENT AND JOHN ADAMS, OF NORTHERN MASSACHUSETTS, BECAME VICE PRESIDENT. SECOND, HE HAD BEEN SPEAKER OF THE PENNSYLVANIA ASSEMBLY AND HAD A RESOUNDING VOICE. HOWEVER, IN 1796, HE CAST THE DECIDING VOTE IN FAVOR OF AN UNPOPULAR TREATY WITH GREAT BRITAIN. THAT NOT ONLY COST HIM HIS SEAT IN THE HOUSE BUT ALSO LED HIS BROTHER-IN-LAW TO STAB HIM.

WE THE PEOPLE

★ FREDERICK MUHLENBERG ★

first president), "His Most Benign Highness" (favored by John Adams, the second), and "His Highness and the President of the United States of America and Protector of the Rights of the Same" (a windy moniker favored by the Senate).

The House is where wars have been declared, where two presidential elections were decided, and where two other presidents were **impeached**. It was the scene of hearings that forced president Richard Nixon to resign in 1974. Although the House is known as the "lower" chamber and the Senate the "upper" chamber, that has nothing to do with prestige. When Congress first met in 1789, it did so in New York City's Federal Hall. The Senate's meeting room was upstairs and the House's was on the main floor.

As the country grew and citizenship

JOHN RANDOLPH OF VIRGINIA REMAINS ONE OF THE MOST OUTLANDISH AND INDEPENDENT FIGURES IN CONGRESS'S HISTORY. RANDOLPH WORE A FLOOR-LENGTH COAT IN THE HOUSE AND OFTEN BROUGHT HIS LARGE FOX-HOUNDS ONTO THE FLOOR WITH HIM, UNTIL HE RAN AFOUL OF THE SPEAKER. HE ALSO PARTICIPATED IN SEVERAL DUELS. AS CHAIRMAN OF THE WAYS AND MEANS COMMITTEE, HE HELPED REMOVE HOUSE RESISTANCE TO THE LOUISIANA PURCHASE IN 1803. HE WAS AN AMBASSADOR TO RUSSIA IN 1830, AND HE SERVED A BRIEF APPOINTMENT TO THE SENATE. ULTIMATELY, HE SPENT 13 TERMS IN THE HOUSE (AND 1 IN THE SENATE) BEFORE DYING WHILE IN OFFICE IN 1833.

WE THE PEOPLE

★ JOHN RANDOLPH ★

laws changed, the House's membership has changed as well. It's written in the Constitution that there must be 1 representative for every 30,000 people. But even that simple fact was complicated from the very beginning by the issue of slavery. According to the Constitution, a slave counted as only three-fifths of one person. Such math hurt Southern states, where slaves were numerous (but weren't allowed to vote, anyway). It also spotlighted the notion, later regarded as shameful, that slaves were "worth" less than white male property owners.

On April 1, 1789, 30 members gathered for the first session of the House of Representatives. That was the minimum required to have a meeting; difficult travel conditions through wilderness and poor roads delayed the others. Rhode Island and

North Carolina hadn't held elections yet, so they didn't have any representatives to send. Ultimately, the first session's roll call consisted of 65 representatives from 13 states.

After the **census** of 1790, the House grew to 105 members. Ten years later, it swelled to 142. And it kept growing. In the 1830s, there were 240 members. Fifty years later, there were nearly 100 more. By 1910, membership stood at 435. People began to argue that the House was becoming too big. Not only was it too big to work effectively, but it had also outgrown its meeting space at the Capitol. In fact, Congress declined to add members after the 1920

> During the Revolution, the Continental Congress was formed by delegates from the colonies.

BUILDING THE HOUSE

census despite its Constitutional requirement to do so. In 1929, Congress passed a law capping the number of representatives at 435. Today, that means that each House member represents about 700,000 people. California has 53 representatives, the most of any state. Texas has the second-most at 36. Alaska, Delaware, Montana, North Dakota, South Dakota, Vermont, and Wyoming have one apiece. Every 10 years, after the census tracks population, some states gain representatives and others lose, but the overall size of the House remains steady.

Some political analysts and groups such as thirty-thousand.org think there should be more members. With each representative serving smaller groups of people, they might be more sensitive to their districts' needs. Some advocate a principle known as the Wyoming Rule that would make all congressional districts roughly as populous as the state of Wyoming. As the least-populated state in the Union (with about 584,000 people), it has just one representative. Enacting such a policy would add about 100 members to the House.

Because representatives are elected every two years, the House membership changes at that rate. Each two-year period marks the beginning of a new Congress, which meets in several sessions until the next group takes office. The Congress that met in 2013 and 2014 for example, was the 113th Congress—the 113th to meet since the first one in 1789–91.

Travel in the late 1700s was difficult

Under the Wyoming Rule, New York City (bottom) would have 34 congressional districts, or 33 more representatives than the state of Wyoming (top).

THE FIRST UNITED STATES CONGRESS, 1789–91

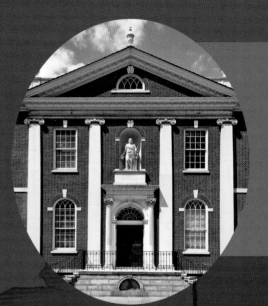

AT FEDERAL HALL
New York City, New York

SESSION 1: March 4, 1789–September 29, 1789
SESSION 2: January 4, 1790–August 12, 1790

AT CONGRESS HALL
Philadelphia, Pennsylvania

SESSION 3: December 6, 1790–March 3, 1791

The **RESIDENCE ACT OF 1790** made Philadelphia the nation's temporary capital city.

BUILDING THE HOUSE

and time-consuming, so representatives traveled back and forth between their home districts and the capital only a few times a year. When they did meet, it was often for six days a week. The long separations from home and family, the heavy workload, and low pay—$6 per day—were serious drawbacks to the job in the early Congresses. In addition, when the government moved from Philadelphia to Washington, D.C. in 1800, congressmen found the new, planned capital city to be little more than a cluster of shacks and crummy rooming houses amid muddy streets. As a result, many House members didn't serve multiple terms, preferring to seek other opportunities in the rapidly growing country. By contrast, representative John Dingell of Michigan retired in 2015 after 59 years in the House. That's the longest anyone has ever served in either chamber.

The first Congress met in three sessions separated by several months-long breaks from 1789 to 1791. The 113th Congress met fairly steadily from 2013 until 2015, but at the most it worked four days a week. For their efforts, representatives in the 113th Congress were paid $174,000. Speaker John Boehner made $223,500.

Congress met in Philadelphia for 10 years before moving to its permanent location, the U.S. Capitol, on November 17, 1800.

HOUSE MEMBER REQUIREMENTS

BE A RESIDENT OF THE STATE THEY REPRESENT AT THE TIME OF THE ELECTION

HAVE BEEN A CITIZEN OF THE UNITED STATES FOR THE PAST ★ 7 ★ YEARS

BE AT LEAST 25 YEARS OLD

CHAPTER 2

A CAST OF THOUSANDS

THE U.S. HOUSE OF REPRESENTATIVES

All that the Constitution requires of a House member is that he or she be 25 years old, a U.S. citizen for at least 7 years, and a resident of the state (but not necessarily the district) he or she represents. Since 1789, more than 10,000 individuals have been elected to the House. Collectively, they have helped shaped the course of history. They've accepted slavery, then outlawed it. They were fractured by the **secession** of Southern states and the Civil War, then rebuilt the Union. They authorized the War of 1812, the Mexican-American War, the Spanish-American War, and U.S. involvement in World Wars I and II. Their legislation created **Prohibition**, then ended it. They took the lead in promoting voting rights for women and minorities.

JONATHAN CILLEY

★ In 1838, ... William Graves of Kentucky killed Jonathan Cilley of Maine in a duel. The next year, Congress banned dueling in the District of Columbia. ★

A CAST OF THOUSANDS

The early House had some customs that wouldn't be allowed today. In the first half of the 19th century, when members were all men, they would frequently send gifts of food, flowers, and other treats to women watching from the galleries. The gifts were delivered on a pole. Also during those years, a rum-based beverage was available to members on the House floor.

But the House wasn't always a friendly home. In 1808, Barent Gardinier of New York and George Campbell of Tennessee argued so intensely over an **embargo** that they challenged one another to a duel with pistols. Campbell wounded Gardinier but did not kill him. In fact, Gardinier later remarked that he should receive a pension for being wounded in service to his country. In 1826, the lively and strong-willed Virginian John Randolph dueled with Henry Clay of Kentucky. Neither was injured. In 1838, though, William Graves of Kentucky killed Jonathan Cilley of Maine in a duel. The next year, Congress banned dueling in the District of Columbia.

The Speaker of the House holds a special position. He or she is second in line to become president if the sitting president dies, resigns, is removed, or is otherwise deemed incapable of serving. Only the vice president stands ahead of the Speaker. The Speaker decides who will lead the House's dozens of committees and which bills go to the committees for discussion. The Speaker also determines when bills will come up for votes before the

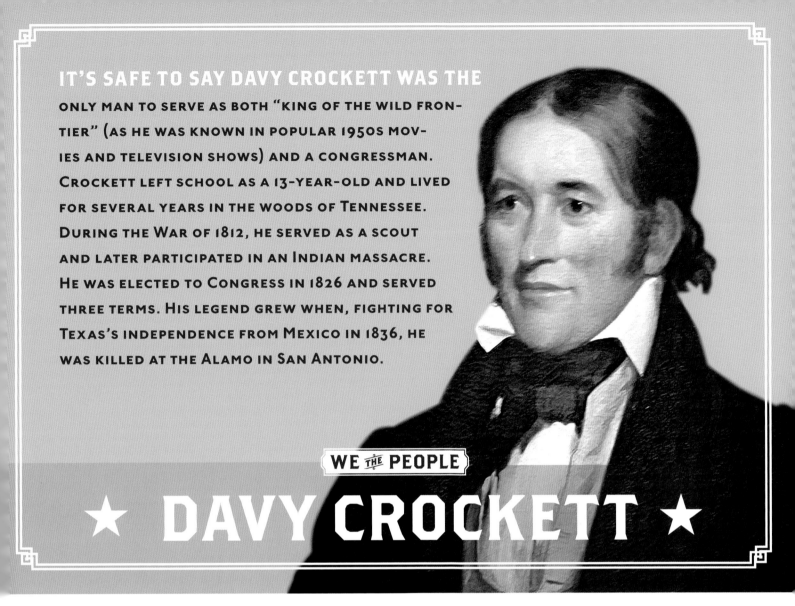

IT'S SAFE TO SAY DAVY CROCKETT WAS THE ONLY MAN TO SERVE AS BOTH "KING OF THE WILD FRONTIER" (AS HE WAS KNOWN IN POPULAR 1950S MOVIES AND TELEVISION SHOWS) AND A CONGRESSMAN. CROCKETT LEFT SCHOOL AS A 13-YEAR-OLD AND LIVED FOR SEVERAL YEARS IN THE WOODS OF TENNESSEE. DURING THE WAR OF 1812, HE SERVED AS A SCOUT AND LATER PARTICIPATED IN AN INDIAN MASSACRE. HE WAS ELECTED TO CONGRESS IN 1826 AND SERVED THREE TERMS. HIS LEGEND GREW WHEN, FIGHTING FOR TEXAS'S INDEPENDENCE FROM MEXICO IN 1836, HE WAS KILLED AT THE ALAMO IN SAN ANTONIO.

WE THE PEOPLE

★ DAVY CROCKETT ★

entire House. However, Speakers seldom weigh in on debates and rarely vote on bills.

Henry Clay is regarded as one of the most important Speakers in history. The Kentuckian had already served a term in the Senate when he was elected to the House in 1811. He encouraged returning to war with Great Britain, this time for interfering with American shipping at sea. After the War of 1812, Clay was part of the U.S. delegation to draw up a peace treaty in Ghent, Belgium. Clay served until 1825 in the House and again in the Senate until 1852. In 1820, he helped fashion the Missouri Compromise. This agreement admitted Missouri as a state that permitted slavery while restricting slavery elsewhere in the former Louisiana Territory. In 1850, Clay worked to have California admitted as a free (non-slave) state, in exchange for Northerners having to return runaway slaves

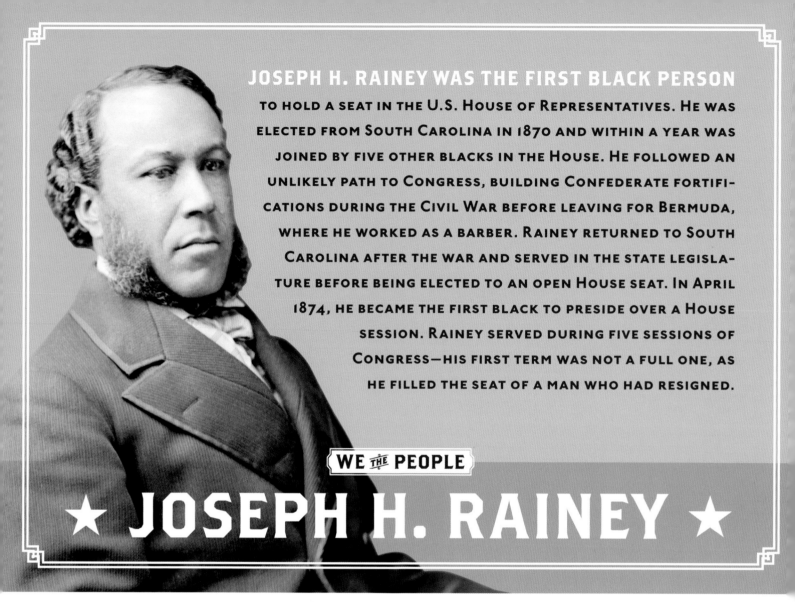

JOSEPH H. RAINEY WAS THE FIRST BLACK PERSON TO HOLD A SEAT IN THE U.S. HOUSE OF REPRESENTATIVES. HE WAS ELECTED FROM SOUTH CAROLINA IN 1870 AND WITHIN A YEAR WAS JOINED BY FIVE OTHER BLACKS IN THE HOUSE. HE FOLLOWED AN UNLIKELY PATH TO CONGRESS, BUILDING CONFEDERATE FORTIFICATIONS DURING THE CIVIL WAR BEFORE LEAVING FOR BERMUDA, WHERE HE WORKED AS A BARBER. RAINEY RETURNED TO SOUTH CAROLINA AFTER THE WAR AND SERVED IN THE STATE LEGISLATURE BEFORE BEING ELECTED TO AN OPEN HOUSE SEAT. IN APRIL 1874, HE BECAME THE FIRST BLACK TO PRESIDE OVER A HOUSE SESSION. RAINEY SERVED DURING FIVE SESSIONS OF CONGRESS—HIS FIRST TERM WAS NOT A FULL ONE, AS HE FILLED THE SEAT OF A MAN WHO HAD RESIGNED.

WE THE PEOPLE

★ JOSEPH H. RAINEY ★

to their owners. After Clay's death, president Abraham Lincoln said the statesman "spoke . . . for the Union, the Constitution, and the freedom of Mankind."

The chair, or leader, of the House Ways and Means Committee is another of the most powerful people in Congress. One of the first committees formed in 1789, the Ways and Means Committee writes the bills establishing taxes.

Thaddeus Stevens of Pennsylvania was chairman of that committee from 1861 through 1865. Stevens, a fierce opponent of slavery, oversaw the financing of the Union's Civil War effort and formed another committee to review how Lincoln was managing it. (At one point, the committee even investigated whether Lincoln's wife, Mary, was a Confederate spy.) Stevens also helped engineer a bill that recruited 150,000

black soldiers. After Lincoln's assassination in 1865, Stevens challenged president Andrew Johnson's plans for **Reconstruction**, which led the House to bring impeachment charges against Johnson in 1867. The Senate's impeachment vote, which failed by one, saved Johnson's presidency. In 2006, historian Robert Remini wrote, "One of the most unique, controversial, determined, and complicated leaders in the entire history of the House of Representatives, [Stevens] was typical of many congressmen, before and after, who were miserable human beings and yet devoted and brilliant legislators."

Thomas Reed of Maine served three

Black soldiers made up about 10 percent of the Union Army during the Civil War.

THOMAS REED

★ [Thomas Reed] earned the nickname "Czar" after he permanently changed the rules on voting in the House. ★

A CAST OF THOUSANDS

terms at the end of the 19th century as Speaker. He earned the nickname "**Czar**" after he permanently changed the rules on voting in the House. Joseph Cannon, who served 46 years in the House and was Speaker shortly after Reed, sought to increase the House's power against the Senate and the presidency. The Cannon House Office Building, where representatives work when they're not on the House floor, was named for him.

President Franklin D. Roosevelt's New Deal, the Vietnam conflict, and the Nixon **Watergate scandal** all shone bright

Part of the New Deal, the Works Progress Administration (WPA) paid people a monthly wage to help build public structures.

spotlights on the House in the 20th century. Sam Rayburn of Texas ushered much of the New Deal through the House as chairman of the Interstate and Foreign Commerce Committee from 1931 to 1937. Then, as Speaker during World War II, he managed to keep secret the billions of dollars spent developing the atomic bomb. Rayburn served 17 years as Speaker—the longest anyone has ever held the job.

During the Vietnam conflict, the House never declared war, one of its key Constitutional powers. As a result, the House passed the War Powers Act in 1973.

HOUSE OF REPRESENTATIVES LEADERSHIP

SPEAKER OF THE HOUSE

Elected by the members of the House, the Speaker presides over both the House and joint sessions of Congress. The Speaker administers the oath of office to House members, enforces House rules, determines the House legislative agenda, appoints representatives to committees, and nominates committee chairpersons.

MAJORITY AND MINORITY LEADERS

Each party elects a leader to serve as its spokesperson. The majority leader represents the party with the most members; the party with fewer members is represented by the minority leader. The majority leader schedules the legislative agenda and the minority leader ensures the policies of the minority group are addressed.

MAJORITY AND MINORITY WHIPS

Each whip tracks the number of votes their party has (and needs) to pass or block a bill. They encourage members to vote in support of the party and ensure that members are present for the session. Whips also serve as the main line of communication between the party leader and other party members.

HOUSE OF REPRESENTATIVES OFFICERS

CLERK OF THE HOUSE

As the record keeper, the clerk conducts roll call, prepares and distributes reports to House members, and maintains a record of all resolutions and documents produced by the House.

CHIEF ADMINISTRATIVE OFFICER

The chief administrative officer manages the administrative and financial aspects of the House, including asset management, information technology, the operating budget, and payroll.

SERGEANT AT ARMS

The sergeant at arms is responsible for safety, security, and order on the House floor. The sergeant may remove disruptive members and compel absent members to the House floor.

CHAPLAIN

The House chaplain opens each meeting with a prayer and provides counseling and spiritual services to House members, family, and staff. The chaplain may also arrange memorial services for the House.

RICHARD NIXON

This act stated that the president would have to consult with the House before committing troops to battle again. President Nixon **vetoed** the measure, but the House and Senate voted to **override** it. Around the same time, the House conducted hearings into Nixon's connections to a burglary that took place in 1972. It occurred at the Democratic National Committee's headquarters at Washington, D.C.'s Watergate Hotel. The American public was riveted to television coverage of the hearings. As the House prepared to impeach Nixon, he resigned, the first president to do so.

The House was a whites-only institution until six blacks from the South were elected in 1870. Membership was male-only until Jeannette Rankin of Montana was elected in 1916. From then on, the number of female representatives climbed slowly but steadily. However, in 1993, the number of women in the House jumped from 29 to 47, reaching a new peak of 84 in 2015. Of the 44 African Americans, 18 were women. Nine of the 32 Hispanics were women, as were 7 of the 13 members described as Asian or Pacific Islander. In 2007, the House elected Nancy Pelosi of California to the first of two terms as Speaker, making her not only the first female Speaker in history but also the highest-ranking woman in American politics.

> Elections are held at the beginning of each Congress to fill House leadership roles and officer positions.

The bill is introduced to the House.

The bill is introduced to the Senate.

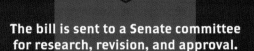

The bill is sent to a House committee for research, revision, and approval.

The bill is sent to a Senate committee for research, revision, and approval.

HOW A BILL BECOMES LAW

Representatives debate the bill and recommend changes.

Senators debate the bill and recommend changes.

The House votes on the revised bill.

If the bill passes, a congressional committee writes a compromise bill to send back through the House and Senate for approval.

The Senate votes on the revised bill.

After both the House and Senate vote to pass the bill, it is sent to the president.

The president signs the bill into law or vetoes it.

CHAPTER 3

THE JOB DESCRIPTION

THE U.S. HOUSE OF REPRESENTATIVES

Accoring to the Constitution, there are three things that only the House of Representatives can do: It can draw up the bills that outline how the government will raise and spend money. It can decide a presidential election, if the Electoral College can't drum up a majority of votes for one candidate. And it can initiate the impeachment process for a president, member of Congress, judge, or other federal official. (The Senate determines whether the impeachment should be carried out.)

It's also the House's job—along with the Senate—to make laws. Congress passes laws, the president signs them, and courts decide whether they're legal. Of course, none of those things is simple. And as a result, the House is a very complicated place.

★ **In reality, a House bill first has to travel through committees that deal with its particular subject. Those committees can make changes to it, known as amendments.** ★

THE JOB DESCRIPTION

The path a bill takes to become a law seems straightforward enough. A member of the House proposes it, and the rest of the House approves it. Then it goes to the Senate, where a majority of the 100 members must approve it before sending it to the president. In theory, the president says, "That's just what I was thinking!" and signs the bill, making it a law. (Bills can also start in the Senate. They must go to the House for approval before going to the president.)

In reality, a House bill first has to travel through committees that deal with its particular subject. Those committees can make changes to it, known as amendments. If the bill requires the government to spend

money, it will have to be examined by several other committees. If a committee chairman doesn't like a bill, he or she can simply refuse to have the committee discuss it. That basically kills the bill for that session of Congress. But if and when the bill reaches the floor of the House, any member can make amendments. Then those have to be approved by a majority of members. The Senate can also make changes. Then the amended bill goes to a committee made up of both House and Senate members. This conference committee irons out the differences. The bill finally travels back to both houses for approval before heading to the president's desk.

In the end, the president can reject

JEANNETTE RANKIN WAS INSTRUMENTAL IN WINNING THE RIGHT TO VOTE FOR WOMEN IN BOTH WASHINGTON STATE AND MONTANA BEFORE SHE BECAME THE FIRST CONGRESSWOMAN. IN CONGRESS, SHE HELPED PASS THE 19TH AMENDMENT TO THE CONSTITUTION, WHICH GRANTED ALL U.S. WOMEN THE RIGHT TO VOTE. RANKIN WAS ALSO A NOTABLE PACIFIST. IN HER FIRST TERM, SHE VOTED AGAINST U.S. INVOLVEMENT IN WORLD WAR I, THEN, BACK IN THE HOUSE IN 1941, VOTED AGAINST INVOLVEMENT IN WORLD WAR II. THE VOTE WAS 388–1. RANKIN LATER SAID SHE WANTED TO BE REMEMBERED MOST FOR HER WORK ACHIEVING VOTING RIGHTS FOR WOMEN.

WE THE PEOPLE

★ JEANNETTE RANKIN ★

the bill. But if the House and Senate feel strongly enough about the bill, they can try to override the veto. To do this, they need the approval of two-thirds of their members. If they get the votes, the bill becomes a law without the president's signature.

The House of Representatives has 21 committees. Most committees examine, debate, and vote on bills in specific subject areas. These include agriculture, the budget, foreign affairs, natural resources, business, and transportation. The Rules Committee, the first one established, is the most powerful committee in the House. It determines the importance of bills and how they'll be debated in the House. Several other committees are "joint" committees, made up of both House and Senate members. Most committees have several subcommittees, which deal with narrower

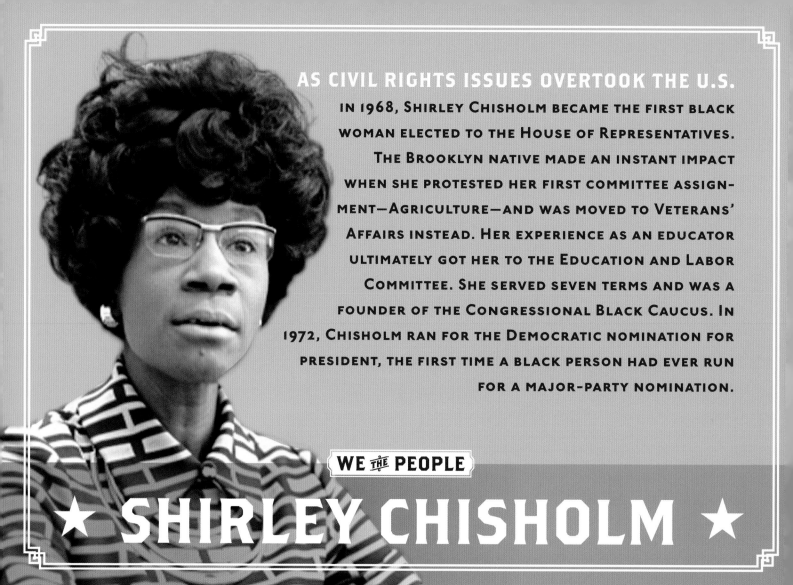

AS CIVIL RIGHTS ISSUES OVERTOOK THE U.S. IN 1968, SHIRLEY CHISHOLM BECAME THE FIRST BLACK WOMAN ELECTED TO THE HOUSE OF REPRESENTATIVES. THE BROOKLYN NATIVE MADE AN INSTANT IMPACT WHEN SHE PROTESTED HER FIRST COMMITTEE ASSIGNMENT—AGRICULTURE—AND WAS MOVED TO VETERANS' AFFAIRS INSTEAD. HER EXPERIENCE AS AN EDUCATOR ULTIMATELY GOT HER TO THE EDUCATION AND LABOR COMMITTEE. SHE SERVED SEVEN TERMS AND WAS A FOUNDER OF THE CONGRESSIONAL BLACK CAUCUS. IN 1972, CHISHOLM RAN FOR THE DEMOCRATIC NOMINATION FOR PRESIDENT, THE FIRST TIME A BLACK PERSON HAD EVER RUN FOR A MAJOR-PARTY NOMINATION.

WE THE PEOPLE

★ SHIRLEY CHISHOLM ★

segments of Americans' lives and government responsibilities. The Natural Resources Committee, for example, has a subcommittee on Indian, Insular, and Alaska Native Affairs. The Transportation and Infrastructure Committee has one subcommittee on the Coast Guard and Maritime Transportation and another dealing with Economic Development, Public Buildings, and Emergency Management.

There are more than 100 House subcommittees in all.

Visitors to the House of Representatives aren't likely to see the 435 members debating on the House floor. With so much work being done in committees, representatives are seldom all in the House chamber. They spend much of their time in their offices meeting with other officials, **lobbyists**, or people from their districts. Members

gather once in the morning for a prayer and to say the Pledge of Allegiance, and they come together for votes. Otherwise, the chamber is often empty. Members of the House can almost always be seen on television giving a speech or discussing policy on the floor, but the television cameras do not show that most of the seats surrounding the speechmaker are usually empty.

The House chamber is also used for the president's State of the Union address.

House members also spend much of their time simply trying to keep their job. All 435 seats in the House open up every 2 years. In modern times, with so much attention from the news and social media, members campaign for

★ The power of impeachment was one the House exercised soon after it was organized. ★

reelection almost constantly. They keep in close contact with supporters, always asking for money. As journalist Sidney Blumenthal first described it in his 1980 book, *The Permanent Campaign*, this state of being in constant campaign mode has forced officeholders—especially House members—to pay too much attention to decisions and publicity with short-term impact.

The power of impeachment was one the House exercised soon after it was organized. It drew up a case for the removal of Tennessee senator William Blount in

> The only senator ever to be impeached by the House, William Blount refused to return to the capital for his Senate trial.

1797. Blount was accused of working with the British to finance military expeditions in the Spanish-held territories of Florida and Louisiana. The Senate expelled him.

A few years later, the House impeached a federal district court judge, John Pickering of New Hampshire, for "improper conduct, mental instability, and intoxication." The Senate tossed him out, too. But when president Thomas Jefferson **cited** Supreme Court justice Samuel Chase for delivering political speeches to grand juries, the Senate decided that judges should not be restricted

EXPELLED REPRESENTATIVES

JOHN B. CLARK

Expelled in 1861
for taking up arms
against the Union

JOHN W. REID

Expelled in 1861
for taking up arms
against the Union

HENRY C. BURNETT

Expelled in 1861
for taking up arms
against the Union

MICHAEL J. MYERS

Expelled in 1980
for involvement in
public corruption scandal

JAMES TRAFICANT

Expelled in 2002
for bribery and other
corruption charges

Of the 20 congressmen expelled from the Senate and the
House, 17 were kicked out for supporting the Confederacy.

CHARLES RANGEL

THE JOB DESCRIPTION

from speaking on issues. Chase's actions weren't deemed "high crimes and misdemeanors," the usual standard for removal from office.

Only two presidents have been impeached by the House—Andrew Johnson, for his strategies during Reconstruction after the Civil War, and Bill Clinton, for lying to investigators who were looking into a sexual affair he'd had. Neither was convicted by the Senate, however, meaning they both remained in office.

Meanwhile, both the House and Senate have often had to discipline their own members. The cases have usually involved some type of financial fraud or bribery, or

> Despite being censured, Charles Rangel was reelected to several more terms by his congressional district in New York.

attempts to influence an election. There are several levels of punishment for such findings. Only five members of the House have been expelled—the most serious penalty. Three were thrown out in 1861 for supporting the Confederacy. Michael J. Myers of Pennsylvania was expelled in 1980 for receiving bribes. In 2002, Jim Traficant of Ohio was expelled after he was convicted on numerous counts of bribery, tax evasion, and other crimes. Twenty-three representatives have been censured, which is a mark of strong disapproval. The most recent censure (in 2010) was against Charles Rangel of New York, for improper fundraising methods and other financial misdeeds.

DISHONEST

BUDGET DEFICIT

LACK OF TRANSPARENCY

NOT GETTING ANYTHING DONE

CATER TO BIG BUSINESS

NOT HELPING

PARTY GRIDLOCK

TAKE TOO MANY VACATIONS

NOT ACCOUNTABLE

CARE TOO MUCH ABOUT POLITICS
NOT ENOUGH ABOUT THE COUNTRY

CHAPTER 4

GRIDLOCK AS USUAL?

THE U.S. HOUSE OF REPRESENTATIVES

I n recent years, the majorities in both the House and the Senate have swung narrowly between Republicans and Democrats. During that time, an intense **partisanship** has resulted in temporary government shutdowns and **stalemates** that have caused Congress's approval ratings to sink. In 2013, a Gallup opinion poll of American adults found that only 14 percent approved of the job Congress was doing. That was the lowest in 40 years' worth of polling. (Polls on Congress were not taken in 1984 and 1985.)

Longtime Washington political analysts Thomas Mann and Norman Ornstein have recently observed that Congress has not produced strong leaders willing to assert their powers in ways befitting its status as the first branch of government. When the majorities have aligned with the party of the president, they say, the House in particular has simply become an agent of the

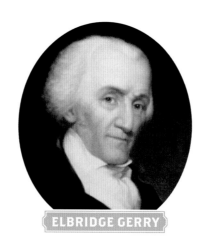

ELBRIDGE GERRY

★ "Congress is designed to stop things, not build them ...
So to block a law is much easier than to pass one." ★

GRIDLOCK AS USUAL?

president, working entirely to promote the president's agenda rather than its own. It has given away its own power for the sake of party loyalty.

Such a strategy won't work, says former California representative Henry Waxman, who served in the House for 40 years until 2015. "Congress is designed to stop things, not build them," Waxman wrote in his 2009 book, *The Waxman Report*. "So to block a law is much easier than to pass one. Moving something forward often requires having the subcommittee chairman, committee chairman, and the Democratic and Republican leadership all be in favor of it, which is rarely the case. If you can find areas of common interest and figure out how to bridge your differences, the result is usually legislation that truly works." Upon his retirement, Waxman told an interviewer that the key to effective legislating is to outlast the opposition. "You keep working. You keep looking for combinations," he said.

Some say an underlying cause of the sense of stalemate, or "gridlock," as it's popularly known, is the regular redrawing of congressional boundaries. Districts are supposed to contain equivalent numbers of people. This ensures that representatives work for roughly the same number of **constituents**. Through much of American history, the district borders didn't change much. But in the 1960s, the Supreme Court determined that they should be redrawn every 10 years

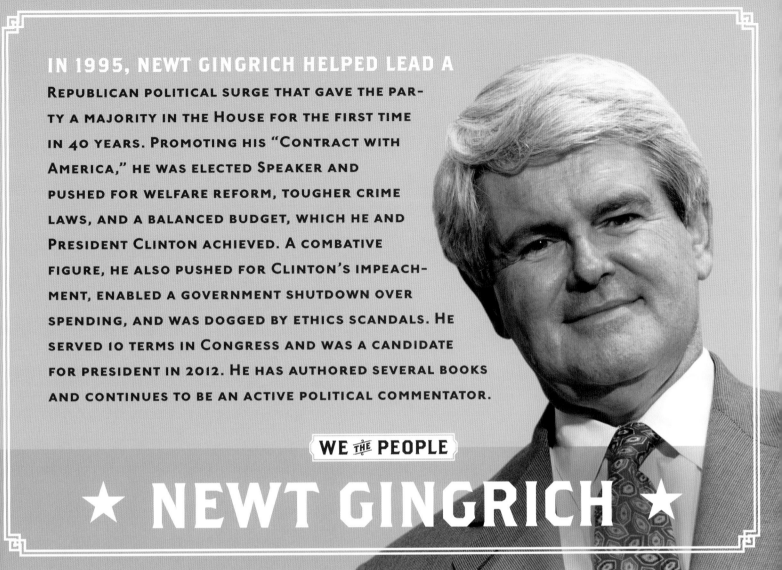

IN 1995, NEWT GINGRICH HELPED LEAD A Republican political surge that gave the party a majority in the House for the first time in 40 years. Promoting his "Contract with America," he was elected Speaker and pushed for welfare reform, tougher crime laws, and a balanced budget, which he and President Clinton achieved. A combative figure, he also pushed for Clinton's impeachment, enabled a government shutdown over spending, and was dogged by ethics scandals. He served 10 terms in Congress and was a candidate for president in 2012. He has authored several books and continues to be an active political commentator.

WE THE PEOPLE

★ NEWT GINGRICH ★

to accommodate changes determined by the national census. Ideally, the districts then would not be heavily weighted toward one political party or the other, or be dominated by particular racial, ethnic, or social groups. They would also be geographically compact.

In reality, the opposite has occurred. Redistricting has often bent a district's borders to enhance the strength of one party or another. The practice even has a colorful name: gerrymandering. It dates back to 1812, when Elbridge Gerry, the governor of Massachusetts, redrew the lines of legislative districts around Boston. Some said the lines made an area that looked like a salamander. *The Boston Gazette* combined the words "Gerry" and "salamander" to make "gerrymandering." When a new district map is challenged in court—as it almost always is—the challengers will likely say it's

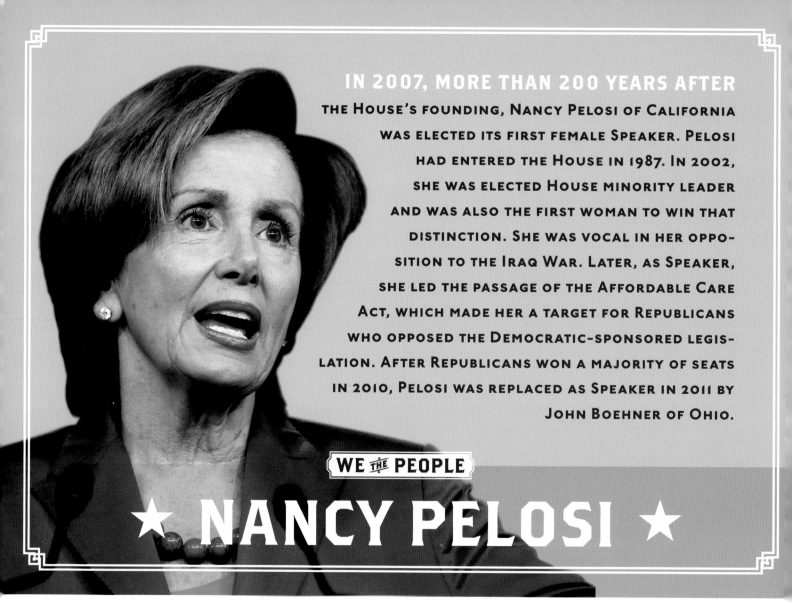

IN 2007, MORE THAN 200 YEARS AFTER THE HOUSE'S FOUNDING, NANCY PELOSI OF CALIFORNIA WAS ELECTED ITS FIRST FEMALE SPEAKER. PELOSI HAD ENTERED THE HOUSE IN 1987. IN 2002, SHE WAS ELECTED HOUSE MINORITY LEADER AND WAS ALSO THE FIRST WOMAN TO WIN THAT DISTINCTION. SHE WAS VOCAL IN HER OPPOSITION TO THE IRAQ WAR. LATER, AS SPEAKER, SHE LED THE PASSAGE OF THE AFFORDABLE CARE ACT, WHICH MADE HER A TARGET FOR REPUBLICANS WHO OPPOSED THE DEMOCRATIC-SPONSORED LEGISLATION. AFTER REPUBLICANS WON A MAJORITY OF SEATS IN 2010, PELOSI WAS REPLACED AS SPEAKER IN 2011 BY JOHN BOEHNER OF OHIO.

WE THE PEOPLE

★ NANCY PELOSI ★

been gerrymandered.

In some states, redistricting is done by independent or bipartisan panels to reduce the chance of legally questionable mapmaking. But in 29 states, redistricting is done by state legislatures. Critics say that partisan interests, coupled with sophisticated mapping and surveying technology, often lead to districting that protects current officeholders by reducing political competition. The

result is a stale Congress. Between 1964 and 2014, more than 80 percent of House members were reelected every 2 years. In 2014, 96.6 percent of current officeholders won reelection to the House. "These days, almost every congressional district is drawn by the ruling party with computer-driven precision to ensure that a clear majority of Democrats or Republicans reside within its borders," Barack Obama wrote in his 2006 book, *The*

Audacity of Hope. "Indeed, it's not a stretch to say that most voters no longer choose their representatives; instead, representatives choose their voters."

Another factor in the low rate of turnover in the House membership is incumbency itself. A big part of a House member's job is to remain visible to his or her constituents, responding to their phone calls, e-mails, and petitions; attending meetings, parades, and barbecues; helping them get over obstacles they might be encountering in the federal **bureaucracy**. Simply by being in office, a House member has a recognizable name, which helps him or her when voters are looking

> Congresspeople must spend a lot of time campaigning if they want to be reelected.

★ However, such contributions can dry up
when Congress is so gridlocked it can't even
keep the government running. ★

the list of candidates on a ballot. Name recognition also helps raise the money it takes to run a campaign. Incumbents often outraise their challengers, attracting big money from independent groups known as political action committees. These groups conduct phone-calling campaigns, buy more billboard ads, and send more mail on the candidates' behalf. "Interest groups ... tend to go with the odds when it comes to political contributions," Obama wrote.

However, such contributions can dry up when Congress is so gridlocked it can't

Political action committees raise money for candidates whom they believe will take their side on legislative issues.

even keep the government running. In 2014, OpenSecrets.org, part of the nonprofit research group known as the Center for Responsive Politics, tracked a decline in the amount of money being spent by lobbyists at the Capitol. It was probing whether lobbying groups had simply found that Congress was a dead end and thus not a wise place to spend money in hopes of changing policies.

In recent years, sharp-eyed visitors to the U.S. Capitol have probably noticed nets collecting pieces that have fallen from the Capitol dome and trays collecting dripping

SALARY of U.S. HOUSE MEMBERS

$6 DAILY	$5,000 ANNUALLY	$96,600 ANNUALLY	$174,000 ANNUALLY
1789	1874	1990	2015

☞ Leaders of the House, such as the Speaker and the majority and minority leaders, are paid a higher salary than other representatives.

STATES with MOST AND LEAST REPRESENTATIVES

CALIFORNIA

ALASKA

DELAWARE

MONTANA

NORTH DAKOTA

SOUTH DAKOTA

VERMONT

WYOMING

 Seven states have only 1 representative in the House, whereas California has 53.

CAPITOL DOME

rainwater. A $60-million repair project began in 2014. For most of two years, the Capitol dome, a shining landmark that in many ways is a symbol of democracy around the world, was to be shrouded in scaffolding.

In the same way, Congress itself might need some structural touch-ups. And some people are thinking about them. A group called FairVote is calling for fewer House districts, but with several representatives in each district—three to five—instead of just one. Voters would choose multiple representatives, which could give a boost to candidates independent of the major parties. FairVote believes such a system could soften the partisanship at the Capitol.

Of course, voters themselves could resolve some of the perceived tangles in Congress by electing majorities in the House and Senate from the same party, with a president to match. But there's not much proof from history that that's been popular. "Gridlock is the regular order," former **House parliamentarian** Charles Johnson said in 2015.

So tension and divisiveness remain part of the House of Representatives, more than 200 years after its creation. That doesn't mean members aren't always striving to make it work better. It only means they're striving to make it work their way.

> The Capitol dome restoration was supervised by the Architect of the Capitol, the office that maintains Capitol Hill's buildings and grounds.

bureaucracy non-elected people who run a government, as well as the departments that employ them

census a count of a population

cited summoned to appear before a court

constituents the people an elected official represents

czar a person with great authority; the title once referred to the emperor of Russia

embargo a government-ordered ban on trade

House parliamentarian someone appointed by the Speaker to manage the Office of the Parliamentarian and advise representatives on all the rules and precedents of the Constitution and House

impeached brought formal charges against a government official for crimes committed while in office

lobbyists people who meet with government officials to try to influence them to support or prevent certain proposals; prohibited from the House floor, lobbyists historically encountered lawmakers in the lobbies

mace a long club with a head

override to cancel

partisanship a fervent bias routinely favoring one group or view over alternatives

Prohibition the period from 1920 to 1933 when the sale, manufacture, importation, and shipping of alcoholic beverages was banned in the United States

Reconstruction the effort in the U.S. between 1865 and 1877 to reorganize the political, legal, and economic systems of the states that had seceded from the Union

secession withdrawal from an alliance

stalemates situations in a contest, dispute, competition, or other interaction in which neither side can gain an advantage or win

vetoed a cancellation by an executive of a measure approved by others

Watergate scandal the events that led to the resignation of president Richard M. Nixon; it began with a burglary at the Watergate Hotel in Washington, D.C.

SELECTED BIBLIOGRAPHY

Draper, Robert. *Do Not Ask What Good We Do: Inside the U.S. House of Representatives*. New York: Simon & Schuster, 2012.

Mann, Thomas E., and Norman J. Ornstein. *The Broken Branch: How Congress Is Failing America and How to Get It Back on Track*. New York: Oxford University Press, 2006.

Obama, Barack. *The Audacity of Hope: Thoughts on Reclaiming the American Dream*. New York: Random House, 2006.

Oleszek, Walter J. *Congressional Procedures and the Policy Process*. 6th ed. Washington, D.C.: Congressional Quarterly Press, 2004.

Remini, Robert V. *The House: The History of the House of Representatives*. New York: Smithsonian Books/HarperCollins, 2006.

Waxman, Henry. *The Waxman Report: How Congress Really Works*. New York: Twelve, 2009.

WEBSITES

Congress for Kids
www.congressforkids.net
Find out more about the branches of government, the Constitution, and elections.

The U.S. House of Representatives
www.house.gov
See what the House is up to in its current events and live floor sessions.

Note: Every effort has been made to ensure that the websites listed above are suitable for children, that they have educational value, and that they contain no inappropriate material. However, because of the nature of the Internet, it is impossible to guarantee that these sites will remain active indefinitely or that their contents will not be altered.

Published by Creative Education and Creative Paperbacks
P.O. Box 227, Mankato, Minnesota 56002
Creative Education and Creative Paperbacks are imprints of The Creative Company
www.thecreativecompany.us

Design and production by Christine Vanderbeek
Art direction by Rita Marshall
Printed in China

Photographs by Alamy (Classic Image, Everett Collection Inc., PARIS PIERCE), Corbis (Bettmann, Blue Lantern Studio, Corbis, LARRY DOWNING/Reuters, Fotofeeling/Westend61, Found Image Press, Rick Friedman/rickfriedman.com, GraphicaArtis, Wally McNamee, Don Troiani), Creative Commons Wikimedia (William R. Birch/U.S. Federal Government, James Bogle and John Vanderlyn, Brady-Handy Collection/Library of Congress, Congressional Pictorial Directory/U.S. Federal Government, Amos Doolittle/Library of Congress, Gentile/Picture History, Chester Harding/Cliff1066, John Wesley Jarvis/Smithsonian's National Portrait Gallery, Library of Congress, Mary A. Livermore, Nixon White House Photographs/NARA, J. B. Sears/Currier & Ives/Library of Congress, Gilbert Stuart, U.S. Government, Joseph Wright/Cliff) Getty Images (John Greim), iStockphoto (VisualField), Shutterstock (Drop of Light, Thiago Leite, Felix Lipov, lkeskinen, VoodooDot)

Library of Congress Cataloging-in-Publication Data
McAuliffe, Bill.
The House of Representatives / Bill McAuliffe.
p. cm. — (By the people)
Includes bibliographical references and index.
Summary: A historical survey of the United States House of Representatives, from its beginnings to present struggles, including its role in Congress and influential members.

ISBN 978-1-60818-675-4 (hardcover)
ISBN 978-1-62832-271-2 (pbk)
ISBN 978-1-56660-711-7 (eBook)
1. United States. Congress. House—Juvenile literature. 2. Legislators—United States—Juvenile literature.

JK1319.M43 2016
328.73/072—dc23   2015039275

CCSS: RI.5.1, 2, 3, 8; RI. 6.1, 2, 4, 7; RH.6-8.3, 4, 5, 6, 7, 8

First Edition HC 9 8 7 6 5 4 3 2 1
First Edition PBK 9 8 7 6 5 4 3 2 1

Pictured on cover: Abraham Lincoln